Diabetic C

Cookbook

Introduction..1

Peanut Butter Cups 2

Sugar-Free Gummy Worms 3

Chocolate Almond Clusters..4

Mocha Meringues 5

Apple-Caramel Crunch Balls 6

Coconut Peanut Butter Balls 7

Butter Candy 8

Soda Cracker Candy...9

Cinnamon Peanut Candy 10

Peanut Butter Candy 11

Cereal Candy..12

Low Carb Almond Joy Candy Bar..............................13

Sugar-Free Marshmallows 14

Sugar-Free Vanilla Marshmallows 15

White Chocolate Truffles 16

Sugar Free Lollipops 17

Sugar Free Holiday Fudge 18

Peanut Brittle 19

Muddy Buddies 20

Sugar Free Gum Drops 21

Sour Lemon Gum Drops 22

Sugar Free Peppermint Patties 23

Sugar-Free Cream Cheese Candies........................24

Sugar-Free Dark Chocolate Candy Bars 25

Strawberry Candy........................26

Golden Coconut Candy........................27

Hard candy 28

Carob Treats........................29

Rainbow Candy........................30

Chocolate Pumpkin Truffles 31

Peanut Butter Fudge 32

Salted Caramel Cashew Fudge 33

Sugar-Free Lemon Coconut Truffles 34

Sugar-Free Dark Chocolate Candy Bars 35

Sugar-Free Cookie Dough Easter Eggs........................36

Chocolate Covered Buttercream Candy Recipe 37

Sugar Free Mint Chocolate Truffles 38

Sugar Free Homemade Tootsie Rolls 39

Low Carb Sugar Free English Toffee........................40

Sugar Free Caramello Bar........................41

Low Carb Almond Joy Candy Bars........................42

Homemade 3 Musketeers........................44

Sugar Free Chocolate Kisses 46

Sugar Free Gummy Candy........................47

Low Carb Strawberry Margarita Gummy Worms........48

Raspberry Chocolate Gummy Bears 49

Pistachio Truffles..50

Chocolate Peanut Low Carb Candy Bar 51

Homemade Payday Candy Bars....................................52

Cucumber and Lime Gummy Snacks 53

About the Author 54

Other Books by Laura Sommers....................................55

Introduction

Having diabetes can be challenging, especially around holidays such as Valentine's Day, Christmas or Halloween. There are so many delicious candy treats that you want to enjoy.

To help maintain your blood sugar, you need low sugar options of the candy that you want to enjoy such as truffles, chocolate bars and gummies.

This cookbook contains scrumptious low sugar versions of all your favorite candy for those with diabetes and those who just want a low sugar alternative.

Peanut Butter Cups

Ingredients:

1/4 cup chopped peanuts
1 (1-oz.) square unsweetened baking chocolate
1 stick butter
1/3 cup SPLENDA sugar substitute
1 tbsp. half-and-half
4 tbsps. reduced fat peanut butter

Directions:

1. Line 10 muffin cups with paper liners. Sprinkle nuts evenly into muffin cups.
2. In a microwaveable bowl, heat chocolate, butter, and Splenda on HIGH about 1 to 1-1/2 minutes, or until melted. (Do not boil.) Stir in half-and-half and peanut butter.
3. Divide mixture evenly into muffin cups. Freeze until firm. Keep frozen until ready to serve.

Sugar-Free Gummy Worms

Ingredients:

2 packages (4-serving size) sugar-free gelatin (any flavor)
2 (0.13-oz.) envelopes unsweetened soft drink mix* (like Kool-Aid, any flavor)
3/4 oz. (3 envelopes from a 1 oz. box) unflavored gelatin
1 cup boiling water

Directions:

1. Coat an 8-inch square baking dish with cooking spray.*
2. In a medium bowl, combine all the ingredients until dissolved. Pour into the baking dish, cover, and chill for 2 to 3 hours, or until completely set.
3. Cut into 1/4-inch strips to form thin "worms" for serving as is or decorating other treats.

Chocolate Almond Clusters

Ingredients:

2 (2.8-oz.) sugar-free chocolate bars
1 cup almonds, coarsely chopped
1/3 cup almond halves, optional for garnish

Directions:

1. Line a baking sheet with aluminum foil.
2. Chop the chocolate into small pieces and place in a microwave-safe bowl. Microwave until melted, stirring after every 45 seconds to prevent overheating. Remove from the microwave when the chocolate is mostly melted, and continue stirring until its entirely melted and smooth.
3. Add nuts to melted chocolate, and stir until well mixed and all the pieces are coated.
4. Using a tsp., drop small spoonfuls of candy onto the prepared baking sheet. If desired, top each cluster with an almond half before the chocolate sets.
5. Place the candy in the refrigerator for 20 minutes to set the chocolate.

Mocha Meringues

Ingredients:

2 egg whites, room temperature
1/2 tsp. cream of tartar
1/3 cup sugar
1/3 cup confectioners' sugar
1 tbsp. instant coffee granules
1 tbsp. warm water
4 (1-oz.) squares, semi-sweet baking chocolate, chopped

Directions:

1. Preheat oven to 225 degrees F. Line 2 baking sheets with parchment paper.
2. In a bowl with an electric mixer on medium speed, beat egg whites and cream of tartar until soft peaks form. Add sugar, 1 tbsp. at a time, until stiff peaks form and sugar is dissolved. Fold in confectioners' sugar.
3. In a small bowl, stir coffee granules into warm water until dissolved. Gently fold into meringue. Drop by tablespoonfuls onto prepared baking sheets.
4. Bake on bottom oven rack 35 to 40 minutes or until dry. Turn off oven and leave meringues for 45 to 50 minutes, or until dry. Store in an airtight container and do not refrigerate.
5. In a saucepan on lowest heat, melt chocolate, stirring often; do not overheat. Remove from heat and stir until smooth. Dip bottoms of each meringue into chocolate, allowing excess to drip back into saucepan. Place on wax paper-lined baking sheets. Let stand in a cool place until set. Do not refrigerate.

Apple-Caramel Crunch Balls

Ingredients:

1/3 cup reduced fat peanut butter
1/4 cup light margarine
1/4 cup honey
2 cups wheat flakes cereal, coarsely crushed
1/3 cup dried apples, finely chopped
2 tbsps. walnuts, finely chopped
1/8 tsp. apple pie spice
1 tbsp. sugar-free caramel syrup

Directions:

1. In a medium saucepan, combine peanut butter, margarine, and honey. Cook and stir over medium heat until mixture comes to a boil. Remove from heat. Stir in cereal, apples, walnuts, and apple pie spice, until well mixed. Transfer to a small bowl; cover and chill 30 minutes. Divide mixture into 18 portions.
2. Using slightly wet hands, firmly press mixture into balls. Place on a waxed paper-lined baking sheet and refrigerate 15 minutes, or until firm.
3. Drizzle balls with caramel sauce. Chill at least 15 minutes, and serve, or store covered in refrigerator.

Coconut Peanut Butter Balls

Ingredients:

1 1/2 cup crispy rice cereal
1 2/3 cup reduced fat peanut butter
1/2 cup granulated Splenda
3/4 cup unsweetened coconut

Directions:

1. Line a baking sheet with wax paper.
2. In a large bowl, combine rice cereal, peanut butter, and Splenda until well mixed.
3. Pour coconut into a shallow bowl.
4. Using about a tsp. at a time, form mixture into balls and roll in coconut to coat.
5. Place on prepared baking sheet and refrigerate at least 1 hour. Store in an airtight container in refrigerator.

Butter Candy

Ingredients:

3 tsps. Skimmed milk (evaporated and unsweetened)
1/3 cup Margarine or butter
1 cup Artificial sweetener
1 tsp. Vanilla
1/8 tsp. salt
1 lb. Sugar-free chocolate coating
1/4 cup Cocoa powder
1 tsp. Cornstarch

Directions:

1. Blend the artificial sweetener and cornstarch in a mixer and grind them to form a powder.
2. Mix the butter/margarine, salt, vanilla, and cream together to form a paste.
3. Combine the cornstarch mix and cocoa powder, and blend it once again in a food processor.
4. Keep the mixture in the refrigerator for an hour. In the meantime, melt the sugar-free chocolate to coat the candies.
5. Make balls of the same size from the candy paste and dip them in the chocolate coating.
6. Place them on a baking tray and bake for 30 minutes at 350 degrees F.

Soda Cracker Candy

Ingredients:

1 cup Sugar replacement
2 tsps. Honey
1 cup Nuts (chopped)
1 packet salt free Soda crackers
1/2 cup Unsweetened chocolate chips

Directions:

1. Spread an aluminum foil out on a cookie sheet and grease it with a little vegetable oil.
2. Sprinkle a little flour on top of it and then place the crackers on it.
3. Boil the sugar replacement, butter, and honey for two minutes and then pour it over the soda crackers.
4. Sprinkle the finely chopped nuts on top of the mixture and bake it at 350 °F for 5 minutes.
5. Take the cracker candies out of the oven and sprinkle the chocolate chips on top. The chips will melt due to the heat.

Cinnamon Peanut Candy

Ingredients:

2 cups Roasted peanuts
1 tsp. Cinnamon
1/4 cup sugar-free Maple syrup
1 Egg white
1/4 tsp. Salt
1/2 cup (optional) Artificial sweetener

Directions:

1. First, preheat the oven to 350 degrees F.
2. Beat the egg white and add the salt, maple syrup, and cinnamon to it. You can also add the artificial sweetener to give it a sweet taste.
3. Now, dip the roasted peanuts into the egg white and cinnamon mixture and coat them with it.
4. Spread them on a baking sheet that has been greased with vegetable oil and bake them for 25 minutes.
5. You can top the peanut candies with cherries for flavor.
6. These sugar-free candies satisfy your sweet tooth in a healthy way. A little effort from your side keeps your sugar levels at bay and lets you enjoy these sweet treats.

Peanut Butter Candy

Ingredients:

1/4 cup Peanut butter
1 tsp. Cocoa
1 tsp. Wheat germ
6-8 Bread slices
2 tsps. Nuts (chopped)
1 tsp. Peanut oil

Directions:

1. Remove the edges of the bread and let the slices dry overnight. The next day, bake them in the oven for half an hour at 350 °F.
2. Crumble the slices and mix them with the peanut butter, wheat germ, and nuts.
3. Drop a little peanut oil into the mixture. Form round candies and grill them for 2 minutes. They are ready to be eaten.

Cereal Candy

Ingredients:

13 oz Evaporated milk
1 tsp. Artificial sweetener
1 tsp. Vanilla extract
1/4 cup Nuts
1/4 cup Butter
3 tsps. Cocoa
2 1/2 cups Unsweetened cereal crumbs

Directions:

1. Mix the cocoa and milk together. Beat it until the cocoa dissolves completely.
2. Now, add the artificial sweetener, butter, and nuts to the milk-cocoa mixture.
3. Heat a saucepan over medium heat and boil the mixture. Cook it for 2-3 minutes, till it changes to a hard paste.
4. Turn off the heat and add the cereal crumbs to the paste.
5. Thicken the mixture by stirring it a bit, and then roll it to make the candies. Bake these for 30 minutes.
6. Refrigerate the candies overnight if you want to eat them chilled.

Low Carb Almond Joy Candy Bar

Filling Ingredients:

7.6 oz. Nestle table cream or heavy cream
1 cup low carb sugar substitute I used about 1 tsp SweetLeaf stevia drops
1 tbsp. vanilla extract
2 1/2 cups unsweetened shredded coconut
50 unsalted roasted almonds leave these out to make Mounds candy bars
Chocolate Coating:
8 oz. unsweetened baking chocolate I prefer Ghirardelli unsweetened baking chocolate
2 oz. cocoa butter
6 Tbsps. low carb sugar substitute or other sugar substitute
1/4 tsp. stevia concentrated powder
1 tsp. vanilla extract
US Customary – Metric
Low Carb Sweeteners | Keto Sweetener Conversion Chart

Directions:

1. In a large bowl, stir together table cream, sweetener, and vanilla extract. Mix in the unsweetened coconut.
2. Using about one tbsp. of coconut mixture each, form into a log and set onto a parchment paper or silicon mat lined baking sheet.
3. Place two almonds on each log (or omit nuts if making Mounds bars).
4. Put baking sheet of logs into freezer while making chocolate coating.
5. In a chocolate melter or double boiler, melt all chocolate coating ingredients together.
6. Remove the coconut logs from the freezer.
7. Place each coconut almond log on a fork and dip bottom into melted chocolate. Then use a spoon to drizzle chocolate over top and sides until log is completely covered in chocolate.
8. Wipe excess chocolate off bottom of fork on side of melter and then set on non-stick sheet to harden.
9. Repeat steps until each log is covered in chocolate.
10. Place finished sheets of candy in refrigerator.
11. Let sit at least an hour then remove and place in covered container. Store in refrigerator.

Sugar-Free Marshmallows

Ingredients:

2 tbsp Unflavored gelatin powder
1 cup Water (warm, divided)
1 1/2 cup Powdered erythritol
1/2 tsp Vanilla liquid stevia
1/4 tsp Sea salt
2 tsp Vanilla extract

Directions:

1. Line an 8x8 in (20x20 cm) pan with parchment paper. Set aside.
2. Pour 1/2 cup (118 mL) warm water into a large bowl (it will barely cover the bottom of the bowl). Sprinkle gelatin over the water and whisk immediately. Set aside.
3. Meanwhile, add remaining 1/2 cup (118 mL) water, powdered erythritol, stevia, and sea salt to a large saucepan. Heat over low to medium heat for a few minutes, stirring frequently, until the mixture is hot, but not boiling, and sweetener dissolves. (The color will change from opaque to slightly translucent, and remove immediately as soon as you see bubbles starting to form at the edges.)
4. Remove from heat. Stir in vanilla extract. Pour the hot liquid into the large bowl with gelatin, while whisking constantly.
5. Using a hand mixer on high power, beat the mixture for about 12-15 minutes, until the volume doubles and the mixture looks very fluffy, like stiff egg white peaks.
6. Transfer the marshmallow mixture into the prepared pan.
7. Refrigerate for at least 8 hours, or overnight, until firm and no longer sticky. Use a sharp chef's knife to cut into squares.

Sugar-Free Vanilla Marshmallows

Ingredients:

1 cup water
3/4 tsp liquid stevia
3 tbsps. gelatin
1 tsp. vanilla extract
1/4–1/2 tsp. vanilla bean

Directions:

1. Place the 3 tbsp of gelatin into the bowl of a stand mixer along with 1/2 cup water.
2. Mix together. Let sit for 5-10 minutes.
3. Have the whisk attachment standing by. **you could use a hand mixer for this
4. Next step you can do in a small saucepan. Heat up 1/2 cup water over medium high heat or heat up the 1/2 cup water in the microwave. Basically you are looking for just about boiling water.
5. Begin to heat the water. Once the water reaches just about boiling temperature immediately remove from the heat.
6. Turn the mixer on low speed and, while running, slowly pour the hot water down the side of the bowl into the gelatin mixture.
7. Once you have added all of the water, add in vanilla extract and vanilla bean powder and liquid stevia and increase the speed to medium-high.
8. Beat at medium-high for 1-2 minutes then increase speed to high.
9. Continue to whip until the mixture becomes slightly thick, approximately 8-10 minutes.
10. While the mixture is whipping prepare the pans as follows.
11. We used a bread loaf pan. You can use anything you like. Lightly grease your pan with some coconut oil (which is what we do). You could put down wax paper instead if you wanted.
12. Once your marshmallow mixture is starting to look like it has some body to it (almost forming peaks), pour the mixture into the prepared pan, using a spatula for spreading.
13. Allow the marshmallows to sit uncovered for a few hours.
14. Once marshmallows have set for a few hours you can start to cut into desired shapes using a sharp knife.
15. Store in an airtight container.

White Chocolate Truffles

Filling Ingredients:

1/2 cup coconut butter
1/2 cup mascarpone cheese
1/3 cup Sukrin Melis or other powdered sweetener
1 scoop unflavored whey protein about 1/3 cup
1 tsps. vanilla extract

Chocolate Coating Directions:

4 oz unsweetened baking chocolate
1 oz cocoa butter food grade
3 tbsps. Sukrin Melis or other powdered sweetener
1/8 tsp. stevia concentrated powder

Filling Directions:

1. Mix together coconut butter, mascarpone cheese, and powdered sweetener on low heat.
2. Remove from heat and stir in whey powder and vanilla extract.
3. Using an electric mixer, beat filling until well combined.
4. Scoop into balls and set on non-stick surface. Shape into balls with hands, if desired.
5. Place in refrigerator for several hours to chill.

Chocolate Coating Directions:

1. Melt baking chocolate, cocoa butter, and powdered sweetener over low heat or double boiler until melted completely.
2. Remove chocolate mixture from heat and stir in stevia and vanilla extracts.
3. Dip chilled balls into chocolate and set on non-stick surface to harden. Drizzle with extra chocolate if desired.
4. Store in refrigerator.

Sugar Free Lollipops

Ingredients:

3 cups sugar-free vanilla syrup
2 cups malitol granular
1 tsp candy flavoring oil
1/4 tsp food coloring
6 candy molds
6 lollipop sticks
Non-stick cooking spray

Directions:

1. Spray the lollipop molds with non-stick cooking spray. Place a lollipop stick in the center of each candy mold.
2. Mix together the malitol and the vanilla syrup in a saucepan. Heat the mixture to a boil over medium heat.
3. Insert a candy thermometer into the liquid while boiling. Keep the mixture boiling until it reaches 300 degrees Fahrenheit. Remove the saucepan from the heat.
4. Stir in the food coloring once the boiling of the liquid has stopped. The food coloring is not required to make the sugar-free lollipops, but makes them look more appetizing.
5. Add your candy flavoring oil to the liquid. Purchase a set with multiple flavors included. Flavor oil examples include chocolate, root beer, butter rum and peppermint. Artificial flavors are used to make the oils and they do not contain sugar. Stir thoroughly.
6. Pour the liquid into each candy mold slowly. The mixture will still be hot so wear gloves to avoid scalding.
7. Remove lollipops from the mold once they have cooled and retain their shapes. Allow them to finish cooling on the countertop.

Sugar Free Holiday Fudge

Ingredients:

1/4 cup butter
2 oz. unsweetened chocolate
24 (1 g) packets Equal sugar substitute
8 oz. cream cheese
1 tsp. vanilla
1/2 cup chopped pecans

Directions:

1. Melt butter in small saucepan, or microwave.
2. Stir in chocolate until melted.
3. Add Equal and vanilla, mixing well.
4. Combine cream cheese and chocolate mixture until it is completely mixed; may use the mixer if you want.
5. Stir in chopped pecans.
6. Spread in an 8-inch square pan that has been greased well with butter.
7. Refrigerate until firm and cut into 1-inch squares. Store in refrigerator.

Peanut Brittle

Ingredients:

1 cup of Roasted & Salted Peanuts
2 oz. of Butter
3 oz. of Swerve
1 tsp. of Vanilla Essence

Directions:

Line a cookie sheet with parchment paper and evenly spread out the peanuts.
Place the butter, swerve and vanilla essence in a small saucepan over medium-high heat.
Cook the mixture to caramel stage, it should be a deep brown color. Note that undercooking the caramel will leave your brittle grainy.
Pour the caramel over the peanuts and leave to cool completely around 30-50 minutes.
Break the cooled brittle into pieces and serve.

Muddy Buddies

Ingredients:

1 1/2 cup pork rinds, broken into bite size pieces
2 oz sugar free semisweet chocolate chips
1 1/4 Tbsp smooth peanut butter
1 Tbsp butter
1/2 tsp vanilla
5T Lakanto Powdered Sweetener

Directions:

Place pork rind pieces into a medium bowl. Put chocolate chips, peanut butter and butter in a small bowl and microwave 30 second or until melted and smooth. Stir in vanilla.

Pour chocolate mixture over the pork rinds and toss to coat them evenly with the chocolate mixture.

Pour coated pork rinds into a large zip top bag and add sweetener. Close bag and shake till pieces are coated well. Pour the coated pork rinds onto a small sheet pan to cool and set. Store them in an airtight container at room temperature.

Sugar Free Gum Drops

Ingredients:

4 Tbsp gelatin (about 6 envelopes)
1 cup cold sweet juice concentrate
1 cup boiling water
1/4 cup apple cider vinegar
1/4 cup lemon juice
1/4 tsp flavored extract (lemon, peppermint, etc.)
1-2 drops food coloring

Directions:

Extra sweetener for coating or a combination of sweetener and citric acid for sour gummies
In a large pot, soften gelatin in cold sweet juice concentrate for five minutes.
Stir in boiling water until gelatin dissolves
Bring to a boil over medium-high heat and boil for 25 minutes. Stir constantly.
Pour mixture into 4 – 3X5 pans.
Add 1/4 tsp extract and 1-2 drops food color to each pan.
Stir until thoroughly combined.
Cover pan and chill overnight in the fridge.
Cut gelatin mixture into 3/4 inch cubes using a knife dipped in hot water.
The gelatin may pull, but continue cutting.
Separate cubes and roll in sugar until coated on all sides.
Place gumdrops on wax paper and leave at room temperature for two days to crystallize.

Sour Lemon Gum Drops

Ingredients:

1/2 cup lemon juice
1/2 cup water
2 tbsp powdered sweetener
3 tbsp gelatin
For Crunchy Coating:
1/2 cup erythritol
1 tsp citric acid (food grade, granular)
8 drops yellow food coloring optional

Directions:

Mix the lemon juice, water and sweetener in a small saucepan over very low heat.
Slowly add the gelatin a little at a time, while stirring.
If you have any chunks, continue to stir until they melt and break down.
Strain the mixture through a wire sieve and into a measuring cup or another vessel with a pouring spout.
Pour the mixture into silicone molds and put in the fridge to set.

Coating Directions:

Transfer the granulated sweetener and citric acid to a glass jar with a lid.
Add food coloring and shake well to combine.
Put gumdrops in the jar, a few at a time, and shake well to coat evenly with the crunchy coating. Transfer the coated gumdrops to a tray and repeat. Do not put all the gummies in the jar at once.

Sugar Free Peppermint Patties

Ingredients:

1/2 cup coconut oil softened
1 tsp. peppermint extract
1 tsps. vanilla liquid stevia
1 tbsp. heavy cream or coconut cream for paleo
Chocolate coating
5 oz. sugar free chocolate chips or 85% dark chocolate
2 tbsps. coconut oil

Directions:

In a blender add all ingredients except chocolate coating ingredients and blend until combined.
Spread evenly into molds or free form small circles on a parchment lined baking pan, making circles 2 inches by 1.5 inches. Freeze patties for 20-30 minutes.
Melt chocolate and coconut oil together in a bowl and mix until smooth.
Remove patties from freezer and mold if used. Dip one patty into melted chocolate at a time using a fork, tap off excess chocolate and place on parchment lined baking pan. Allow to set by refrigerating for 30 minutes. Best if kept refrigerated.

Sugar-Free Cream Cheese Candies

Ingredients:

1 oz natural, unsweetened full-fat cream cheese
1–2 drops pure peppermint oil
1/2 tsp. beetroot juice
1–1 1/2 cups + 1/4 cup powdered erythritol (Confectioner's sugar) for dipping

Directions:

Combine cream cheese, peppermint oil and beetroot juice in a small bowl.
Mix with spoon until well mixed.
Sift the sweetener.
Add the sweetener 1/4 cup (60 ml) at a time and mix well after each addition.
When the mixture is so stiff that you cannot mix it anymore with spoon, knead in the rest of the powdered sweetener, adding it little by little and kneading well after each addition.
Keep adding more sweetener little by little and kneading after each addition until you have reached the right consistency. The right consistency is when the dough is like Play-Doh, so you can mold it easily and it's not sticky, on the other hand it's not too hard and crumbly.
Take tiny balls from the dough. You can place the balls on a parchment paper or waxed paper and flatten them with a fork dipped in powdered sweetener.
Another alternative is to press the tiny balls into molds, just roll the balls thoroughly in powdered sweetener before pressing them into molds.
You can also roll out the dough and cut out tiny heart shapes with a cookie cutter.
Place the candies in the freezer for a couple of hours to harden.

Sugar-Free Dark Chocolate Candy Bars

Ingredients:

4 oz. unsweetened cacao or baking chocolate
3 tbsps. coconut oil
1 tsp. pure vanilla extract
1/4 tsp. salt
2 tbsps. milk
1 tsp. liquid vanilla stevia
1 1/2 tbsps. powdered stevia

Directions:

Melt all ingredients in a sauce pan over low heat on the stove until completely smooth.
Pour into candy mold and refrigerate or freeze until hardened.

Strawberry Candy

Ingredients:

1 (15 oz./500ml) can sweetened condensed milk
1 lb./450gr finely ground coconut
2 (3 oz./100ml) pkgs. strawberry-flavored gelatin, divided (not sugar-free)
1 cup finely ground almonds
7 drops of clear liquid stevia extract
1 tsp. vanilla extract
1 (4 1/2 oz./150ml) can green decorator icing

Directions:

Combine milk, coconut, 1 package gelatin, almonds, stevia, and vanilla; mix well. Shape mixture into strawberries. Roll candies in remaining gelatin, coating thoroughly. Let candies dry until firm. Make leaves with icing on top of candies. Store in a covered container.

Golden Coconut Candy

Ingredients:

2 1/2 cups coconut, shredded
1 1/4 tsps. of white stevia powder
1/2 cup water
1 stick cinnamon
2 tbsps. butter
3 egg yolks
2 cups milk

Directions:

Place coconut on a cookie sheet lined with aluminum foil. Toast for 15 minutes, turning occasionally to brown on all sides. Cool and set aside. Grease an 8-inch square pan, line with parchment paper, then grease the paper. In a large pot, combine stevia, water, cinnamon and butter. Cook over low heat, stirring gently. Cover and cook over medium heat for 2 to 3 minutes. Uncover, stir in shredded coconut and, when it appears transparent, add the egg yolks beaten with the milk. Beat, stirring constantly, until the bottom of the pan is visible. Transfer into the prepared cake pan. Preheat oven to 375Â°F (200Â°C). Bake candy for 45 minutes, or until golden brown. Remove from the oven and let cool for 1 day, then cut into squares.

Hard candy

Ingredients:

1/4 pound butter
1 cup maltitol
6 drops clear liquid stevia extract
1/2 tsp. flavor oil (specific for candy)
Greased candy molds

Directions:

Melt the butter over medium heat in a non-sticky pot. Stir the granulated maltitol into the butter, keeping the mixture on the heat. Stir the mixture continuously until it turns a slightly dark caramel color. Remove the pot from the heat and stir your flavor oil into the mixture. Pour the mixture into your greased candy molds and allow the candy to cool and harden. Wrap the cooled individual candies in wax paper and store in an airtight container.
Coconut carob treats with stevia (recipe courtesy of Casey Lorraine Thomas)

Carob Treats

Ingredients:

1 avocado
4 tbsps. of carob powder
White stevia powder to taste (add enough stevia so that the mixture is a little sweeter than you like. Once you add the coconut and freeze the blobs they won't be quite as sweet)
1 tsp. of vanilla extract
2/3 cup of coconut chips/flakes

Directions:

In a food processor fitted with the "S" blade, process the avocado, carob or cacao, vanilla extract and stevia until well combined, thick and creamy. You will need to stop the processing and scrape the sides of the food processor once or twice. Take the "S" blade out of the food processor and add the coconut chips to the mixture. Mix well with a spoon. Spoon "blobs" of the mixture onto a plate. You can use your hands to shape balls if your prefer.Freeze the blobs for about one hour and then enjoy!
Lemon and coconut balls with stevia (recipe courtesy of Casey Lorraine Thomas)coconut balls with stevia

Rainbow Candy

Ingredients:

8 pkg. unflavored gelatin
16 oz. any fruit flavor sugar-free pop
3 tbsp. liquid sweetener
1 to 1 1/2 tsp. fruit flavoring
Food coloring (if desired)

Directions:

Pour 8 oz. of pop in pan and sprinkle one package gelatin at a time until absorbed. Add rest of pop gradually. Stir and let set until gel is completely softened. Place pan on low heat and stir until all is dissolved. Remove from heat and add sweetener, flavoring and coloring. Pour in jelly roll pan 10 x 15-inches. Set in refrigerator 30 minutes covered. Will be very firm. Cut in desired shapes. Will keep in refrigerator one week.

Chocolate Pumpkin Truffles

Truffle Ingredients:

6 oz. unsweetened baking chocolate
1 tbsp. butter
1/2 cup Swerve
3 oz. cream cheese. softened
1/4 cup pumpkin puree
1 tsp. pumpkin pie spice
3/4 cup dry powdered milk
2 tsps. chocolate or vanilla liquid stevia
Chocolate Coating:
8 oz. unsweetened baking chocolate mixed with 2 tsps. vanilla liquid stevia or
1/4 cup Swerve or use Lily's sugar-free chocolate chips
Optional: coconut sugar for sprinkle

Directions:

1. Melt the chocolate and butter in a microwavable bowl 30 seconds or until melted. Stir until smooth then add Swerve and stir until combined. Set aside to cool.
2. In a stand mixer combine cream cheese and pumpkin and blend until there are no lumps.
3. Add the last 3 ingredients and the cooled chocolate and blend until combined well. Refrigerate until firm about 1 hour.
4. Roll into balls and place on a parchment lined baking sheet.
5. Melt chocolate in a microwavable bowl, add stevia and taste and just to your preference.
6. Roll one truffle at a time in chocolate. Set on baking sheet. Sprinkle with coconut sugar if desired. Store in the refrigerator until ready to serve.

Peanut Butter Fudge

Ingredients:

1 cup unsweetened peanut butter
1 cup coconut oil
1/4 cup unsweetened vanilla almond milk
optional: pinch salt only if your peanut butter is unsalted
optional: 2 tsps. vanilla liquid stevia or desired sweetener to taste
Optional Topping: Chocolate Sauce
1/4 cup unsweetened cocoa powder
2 tbsps. coconut oil melted
2 tbsps. Swerve or sweetener of choice

Directions:

1. Slightly melt or soften the peanut butter and coconut oil together in the microwave or low heat on the stove.
2. Add this to your blender and the rest of the ingredients.
3. Blend until combined.
4. Pour into a parchment lined loaf pan.
5. Refrigerate until set, about 2 hours.
6. If using chocolate sauce, whisk ingredients together and drizzle over fudge after it's been set.
7. Best if kept refrigerated.

Salted Caramel Cashew Fudge

Ingredients:

1/2 cup butter
1/2 cup cashew butter
1 cup Swerve
1 cup Silk UnSweetened Cashew Milk
1 tsp. arrowroot powder
1 tbsp. maple syrup
1 tbsp. molasses
1/2 tsp. toffee liquid stevia
2 1/2 cup sugar free chocolate chips like the brand Lily's
1 tsp. coarse sea salt
1/4 cup cashews

Directions:

1. Melt butter and cashew butter over medium heat in a sauce pan.
2. Once butters are melted stir in Swerve, cashew milk, arrowroot powder, maple syrup, and molasses.
3. Bring mixture to a boil and simmer 3-4 minutes until thickened.
4. Turn off heat and add in liquid stevia and chocolate chips.
5. Stir well until chocolate chips are melted.
6. Pour mixture in to a parchment lined baking pan.
7. Top with cashews and sea salt.
8. Refrigerate 3 to 4 hours or overnight.

Sugar-Free Lemon Coconut Truffles

Ingredients:

4 oz. cream cheese softened
2 tbsps. coconut oil melted
2 tbsps. coconut cream from the can
pinch salt
1 tbsp lemon juice
1-2 tsp lemon liquid stevia or to taste
2 tbsps. coconut shredded, unsweetened
Outer coating
1/2 tbsp. lemon zest
1/4 cup coconut shredded, unsweetened

Directions:

1. In a stand mixer blend the cream cheese and coconut oil until smooth.
2. Blend in the coconut cream, salt, lemon juice and lemon stevia.
3. Taste and adjust lemon juice and stevia to your liking.
4. Stir in shredded coconut and refrigerate mixture for 30 minutes.
5. In a small bowl mix the outer coating ingredients together.
6. Using a 1/2 tbsp., spoon out refrigerated mixture and form into 18 balls rolling each in the coating mixture then placing on a parchment lined baking sheet.
7. Best if kept refrigerated until ready to serve.

Sugar-Free Dark Chocolate Candy Bars

Ingredients:

4 oz. 100 % unsweetened cacao or baking chocolate
3 tbsps. coconut oil
1 tsp. pure vanilla extract
1/4 tsp. salt
2 tbsps. milk of choice
1 tsp. liquid vanilla stevia
1 1/2 tbsps. powdered stevia

Directions:

1. Melt all ingredients in a sauce pan over low heat on the stove until completely smooth.
2. Pour into candy mold and refrigerate or freeze until hardened.

Sugar-Free Cookie Dough Easter Eggs

Ingredients:

1/2 cup butter softened at room temperature
8 oz. cream cheese room temperature
1/4 cup coconut milk unsweetened
1 tsp. coconut liquid stevia
1 tsp. vanilla extract
1/2 tsp. salt
1 cup coconut flour
4 oz. sugar free chocolate chips
Chocolate Coating
8 oz. sugar free chocolate
1 tbsp. butter

Directions:

1. Blend the first six ingredients with an electric mixer until smooth. Taste and adjust sweetener, if needed. Mix in coconut flour, then stir in chocolate chips.
2. Press into Easter egg mold, or shape into ovals, and lay on a parchment-lined baking sheet. Freeze for 30 minutes.
3. Melt chocolate and butter together, then stir until completely smooth. Pour in about 2 tsp. of chocolate into Easter egg mold, then insert frozen cookie dough egg and cover with more chocolate. If you don't have an egg mold, simply dip each oval-shaped cookie dough egg into melted chocolate until covered. Remove with a fork, tapping off excess chocolate and lay onto parchment-lined baking sheet.
4. Refrigerate until chocolate is hardened. Best if kept refrigerated until ready to serve.

Chocolate Covered Buttercream Candy Recipe

Filling Ingredients:

1/4 cup butter softened
1 1/2 oz. cream cheese softened
3/4 tsp. flavored extract (vanilla, orange, maple, lemon, coconut, etc)
1 1/2 cups Swerve Confectioners Powdered Sweetener more or less to taste
Chocolate Coating
4 oz. unsweetened baking chocolate
1 oz. cocoa butter
3 tbsps. Swerve Confectioners Powdered Sweetener
1/8 tsp. stevia concentrated powder
1/2 tsp. vanilla extract

Filling Directions:

Combine butter and cream cheese in large bowl. Beat at medium speed, scraping bowl often, until smooth.
Add vanilla; continue beating until well mixed. Reduce speed to low.
Beat, gradually adding low carb powdered sugar replacement, until well mixed.
Place mixture in refrigerator for about an hour (or at least 10 minutes in freezer) so mix is easier to work with.
Use spoon or cookie scoop to scoop out even sized balls. These can be shaped into squares, made into egg shapes (for Easter), or any other shape desired.
Place shaped filling in freezer while making chocolate coating.

Chocolate Coating Directions:

In a chocolate melter or double boiler, melt all chocolate coating ingredients together.
Remove the shaped filling from the freezer.
Place each on a fork and into melted chocolate until well coated. Wipe excess chocolate off bottom of fork on side of melter and then set on non-stick sheet to harden.
Repeat until each is covered in chocolate.
Place finished sheets of candy in refrigerator.
Let sit at least an hour then remove and place in covered container. Store in refrigerator.

Sugar Free Mint Chocolate Truffles

Ingredients:

1/2 cup heavy cream 125ml
8 Tbsp. butter, unsalted 120ml
12 oz. baking chocolate, unsweetened 340g
1/2 tsp. peppermint extract - just under.
1 tsp. pure stevia extract   "   "
1/4 tsp. salt   "   "
1-1/2 cups chocolate chips, sugar-free 375

Directions:

Over medium low heat, add the cream and butter to a saucepan. Stir it until it melts and the cream simmers. Remove from heat and add in the baking chocolate, stevia, and salt. Stir until all melted and combined well. Pour mixture into a bowl and refrigerate until firm enough to mound into a spoon, about 30 minutes. Line a baking sheet with parchment paper and scoop the chocolate mixture by tbsps.. Cover and refrigerate again for another 30 minutes. Roll each mound until smooth and freeze for 20 minutes. Melt the chocolate chips and dip each truffle in melted chips one at a time. Remove with a fork, shake off excess chocolate, and return to baking sheet. Sprinkle optional pink sprinkles on top. Refrigerate until firm, about 1 hour.

Sugar Free Homemade Tootsie Rolls

Ingredients:

1/4 cup cocoa
1/4 cup unflavored whey protein
2 tbsps. powdered whole milk
1/2 cup powdered low carb sugar substitute
1/8 tsp. pinch salt
60 grams Sukrin Fiber Syrup or other Oligosaccharide syrup
2 tbsps. butter melted
1/2 tsp. vanilla extract

Directions:

Powder granular sweetener in blender or food processor.

Mix cocoa, whey protein powder, powdered milk, low carb sweetener, and salt in medium bowl. Set aside.

Heat fiber syrup in microwave until bubbles form (about 30 seconds). Add melted butter and vanilla.

Stir dry cocoa mix into wet fiber syrup mix until crumbly. Using hands, knead mixture until a dough is formed.

Shape dough into a ball, then flatten out. Cut into strips and roll out each strip into a rope about the diameter of a Tootsie roll. Cut dough rope into Tootsie roll size pieces.

Wrap each roll in small rectangular pieces of wax paper if desired. Store rolls in refrigerator so they will be firm.

Low Carb Sugar Free English Toffee

Ingredients:

3/4 cup Swerve Sweetener
1/2 cup butter
1/2 tsp. vanilla extract
Pinch salt
2 tbsp. powdered Swerve Sweetener
1/2 cup sugar-free dark chocolate chips
1/2 tbsp. butter
1/2 cup toasted chopped macadamia nuts (or other toasted nuts)

Directions:

Line a 9×13 inch pan with foil.
In a medium heavy-duty saucepan over medium heat, combine Swerve and butter and stir until Swerve is dissolved. Bring to a boil and cook without stirring until mixture darkens to a deep amber, about 5 to 7 minutes (time may vary depending on the quality of your cookware).
Remove from heat and stir in vanilla extract and salt. If the mixture appears to be separating, stir in 2 tbsp of powdered Swerve Sweetener until it comes back together. Pour mixture into prepared pan. Let cool completely.
In a bowl set over a pan of barely simmering water, melt chocolate chips and butter together until smooth. Spread over cooled toffee
Sprinkle with chopped nuts and refrigerate until set.

Sugar Free Caramello Bar

Ingredients:

1 cup Swerve confectioners
6 tbsp. organic butter
1/2 cup organic heavy whipping cream

White Chocolate Bar Ingredients:

2 oz. cocoa butter
1/3 cup Swerve confectioners
1 tsp. vanilla (or other extract like mint)
1/8 tsp. Celtic sea salt

Milk Chocolate Bar Ingredients:

Add 1/4 oz. unsweetened baking chocolate

Dark Chocolate Bar Ingredients:

Add 1/2 to 1 oz. unsweetened baking chocolate depending on how dark you like it.

Directions:

Before you begin, make sure you have everything ready to go - the cream and the butter next to the pan, ready to put in. If you don't work fast, the sweetener will burn. Heat butter on high heat in a heavy-bottomed 2-quart or 3-quart saucepan. As soon as it comes to a boil, watch for specks of brown (this is brown butter....SO GOOD on veggies!). Immediately add the Swerve and the cream to the pan. Whisk until caramel sauce is smooth. Let cool in the pan for a couple minutes, then pour into a glass mason jar and let sit to cool to room temperature. Store in the refrigerator for up to 2 weeks.
Place cocoa butter in a double boiler and heat on medium high until fully melted (or microwave safe bowl and heat on high for one minute, check and heat for 30 seconds until melted). Melting cocoa butter takes longer than traditional fats.
Stir in natural sweetener.
Stir in extracts and salt.
Place melted chocolate into candy bar mold, enough to to cover the bottom and sides, and cool in refrigerator until white chocolate is solid, about an hour. Or the speedy method; you can place the molds in a freezer till they are set up, which will only take a couple of minutes versus and hour.
Once cool, fill the divots with caramel and set in freezer to set.
Once the caramel is set, remove from freezer and cover with additional melted chocolate.

Low Carb Almond Joy Candy Bars

Filling Ingredients:

7.6 oz. Nestle table cream or heavy cream
1 cup low carb sugar substitute I used about 1 tsp SweetLeaf stevia drops
1 tbsp. vanilla extract
2 1/2 cups unsweetened shredded coconut
50 unsalted roasted almonds leave these out to make Mounds candy bars
Chocolate Coating:
8 oz. unsweetened baking chocolate I prefer Ghirardelli unsweetened baking chocolate
2 oz. cocoa butter
6 Tbsps. low carb sugar substitute or other sugar substitute
1/4 tsp. stevia concentrated powder
1 tsp. vanilla extract

Directions:

In a large bowl, stir together table cream, sweetener, and vanilla extract. Mix in the unsweetened coconut.
Using about one tbsp. of coconut mixture each, form into a log and set onto a parchment paper or silicon mat lined baking sheet.
Place two almonds on each log (or omit nuts if making Mounds bars).
Put baking sheet of logs into freezer while making chocolate coating.
In a chocolate melter or double boiler, melt all chocolate coating ingredients together.
Remove the coconut logs from the freezer.
Place each coconut almond log on a fork and dip bottom into melted chocolate. Then use a spoon to drizzle chocolate over top and sides until log is completely covered in chocolate.
Wipe excess chocolate off bottom of fork on side of melter and then set on non-stick sheet to harden.
Repeat steps until each log is covered in chocolate.
Place finished sheets of candy in refrigerator.
Let sit at least an hour then remove and place in covered container. Store in refrigerator.

Low Carb Almond Fudge Truffles

Ingredients:

1/2 cup unsweetened cocoa powder
4 oz. cream cheese
1-2 tbsps. heavy cream optional – see note
3 Tbsps. Truvia
1/2 tsp. almond extract or other flavor extract
cocoa powder

Unsweetened coconut
Chopped nuts

Directions:

1. In food processor or mixer, combine 1/2 cup cocoa powder, cream cheese, cream (if using) and almond extract until well blended.
2. Using a small scoop or spoon, divide mixture evenly and roll into balls. Roll balls in desired topping – cocoa, coconut, or chopped nuts.

Homemade 3 Musketeers

White Chocolate Bar Ingredients:

2 oz. cocoa butter
1/3 cup Swerve confectioners
1 tsp. toffee extract or a few drops toffee oil
1/8 tsp Celtic sea salt

Milk Chocolate Bar Ingredients:

Add 1/4 oz. unsweetened baking chocolate

Dark Chocolate Bar Ingredients:

Add 1/2 to 1 oz. unsweetened baking chocolate (depending on how dark you like it)

Filling Ingredients:

1 cup coconut oil or butter, room temperature
1 1/4 cup Swerve confectioners
4 (1 oz.) squares unsweetened baking chocolate, melted and cooled
1 vanilla bean or 1 tsp. vanilla extract
1/4 tsp almond extract
4 eggs

Directions:

1. Place cocoa butter in a double boiler and heat on medium high until fully melted (or microwave safe bowl and heat on high for one minute, check and heat for 30 seconds until melted). Melting cocoa butter takes longer than traditional fats.
2. Stir in natural sweetener.
3. Stir in extracts and salt
4. line the edges of truffle or candy bar mold with the chocolate leaving the center open for the filling to go in and then will put chocolate on top of filling to seal it. If the chocolate won't stay up the edges of the mold to line it, let set up just halfway by cooling it in the freezer for a minute or two and then smooth it around with finger to get the sides lined and ready to set and fill. Sometimes the chocolate is too oily and needs to set up slightly in order to stick to edges of candy mold.
5. Cool in refrigerator until white chocolate is solid, about an hour. Or the speedy method; you can place the molds in a freezer till they are set up, which will only take a couple of minutes versus and hour.

Filling Directions:

1. Cream coconut oil or butter in a mixing bowl. Gradually beat in the natural sweetener with an electric mixer until light colored and well blended. Stir in the thoroughly cooled chocolate, vanilla and almond. Add the eggs, one at a time, beating 5 minutes on medium speed after each addition. Refrigerate at least 2 hours before making candy bars.

Directions:

1. Remove the mold from the fridge or freezer and fill with filling. Then top off the filling with a layer of the cocoa butter mix so that the filling is inside and surrounded by the chocolate. Place back into fridge/freezer to set.

Sugar Free Chocolate Kisses

Ingredients:

4 oz. unsweetened baking chocolate
1 oz. cocoa butter food grade
3 tbsps. Swerve Confectioners Powdered Sweetener or Sukrin Melis
1/8 tsp. stevia concentrated powder
1/2 tsp. vanilla extract

Directions:

1. Melt baking chocolate, cocoa butter, and powdered sweetener over low heat or double boiler until melted completely.
2. Remove chocolate from heat and stir in stevia and vanilla extracts.
3. Pour melted chocolate into molds. Refrigerate or freeze until completely set.
4. Remove chocolate from molds and enjoy.

Sugar Free Gummy Candy

Ingredients:

1/2 cup freshly-squeezed lemon juice
3 Tbsp grass-fed gelatin
30-40 drops liquid stevia (to taste)

Directions:

1. Whisk all ingredients in a small sauce pan.
2. Heat over low heat until mixture loses its "applesauce" consistency and starts to liquify.
3. Pour into molds. (I like to transfer the mixture to an easy-pour container first to avoid spills, especially if you have small molds!)
4. Allow gummies to set. You can either do this by placing molds on a flat surface in the freezer, fridge or on the counter. The freezer is your quickest option and will take about 10-15 minutes to set.
5. Remove from molds and store in the fridge in an air tight container. These will last about two weeks, although the texture becomes firmer over time, they are still delicious!

Low Carb Strawberry Margarita Gummy Worms

Ingredients:

10 hulled strawberries, fresh or frozen
2 oz. silver tequila
3 tbsps. grass-fed gelatin collagen protein
2 tbsps. powdered erythritol
1 1/2 oz. fresh lime juice

Directions:

1. Combine the strawberries and tequila in a blender and pulse until smooth.
2. Pour the strawberry-and-tequila mixture into a medium saucepan and set over low heat. Add the gelatin, erythritol, and lime juice and whisk to dissolve the gelatin and combine the ingredients. Continue to heat for about 10 minutes, whisking frequently, until the mixture becomes pourable. It will start out very thick but will become thinner and smoother as it heats.
3. Transfer the mixture to a measuring cup or a bowl with a pour spout.
4. Quickly pour the mixture into the gummy worm mold and transfer to the refrigerator.
5. Refrigerate for 10 to 15 minutes, until set. Pop the gummy worms out of the mold and enjoy! Store le overs in the refrigerator for up to a week.

Raspberry Chocolate Gummy Bears

Raspberry Gummy Mixture Ingredients:

1/2 cup boiling water
1/2 cup fresh raspberries
2 packets gelatin (0.25 oz. per packet)
10-15 drops liquid stevia

Chocolate Gummy Mixture Ingredients:

1/2 cup boiling water
2 packets gelatin (0.25. oz per packet)
1.5 tbsps. cocoa powder
10-15 drops liquid stevia

Raspberry Gummy Mixture Directions:

1. Add fresh raspberries to boiling water in a bowl. Mash raspberries until all of the juice is released.
2. Using a fine mesh strainer, filter liquid from seeds. Set seeds aside.
3. Check temperature of raspberry liquid. If still warm, add in gelatin a little at a time. Stir well until all clumps are gone.
4. Add in stevia to taste.

Assemble Gummy Bears Directions:

5. Using a heart-shaped gummy bear mold with a dropper, add the raspberry mixture to the molds. If you want some gummies to have both raspberry and chocolate, fill the molds up halfway.
6. Place molds into fridge.

Chocolate Gummy Mixture Directions:

7. To a second bowl, add in more boiling water, and slowly stir in gelatin.
8. Add in cocoa powder and liquid stevia. Stir until well-combined.
9. Remove gummy bear molds from fridge and check that raspberry mixture has hardened.
10. Add chocolate mixture to the molds, and return to the fridge until fully hardened, approximately 15-20 minutes.
11. Remove from molds and add to an air-tight container. Store in fridge for 4-5 days.

Pistachio Truffles

Ingredients:

8 oz. (1 cup) mascarpone cheese, softened
1/4 tsp. pure vanilla extract
3 tbsps. confectioners style erythritol sweetener
1/4 cup chopped pistachios

Directions:

1. In a small bowl, combine the mascarpone, vanilla, and sweetener.
2. Mix gently but thoroughly with a fork or spatula, until well blended and smooth.
3. Roll by hand into 10 balls, about 1 inch in diameter. (if too soft to roll, chill 10 minutes and try again.)
4. Place the pistachios on a small plate and roll the truffles in them until completely coated.
5. Chill 30 minutes before serving.

Chocolate Peanut Low Carb Candy Bar

Ingredients:

1 cup Lily's chocolate chips
2 tbsps. coconut oil
1/2 cup chopped peanuts
Sprinkle coarse salt

Directions:

1. In a microwave safe dish, melt chocolate chips with coconut oil.
2. Using a bar pan, place 1 tbsp. of melted chocolate in each cavity.
3. Sprinkle with chopped peanuts.
4. Cover peanuts with remaining chocolate.
5. Sprinkle with coarse salt, if desired.
6. Place in freezer to harden.
7. Store leftovers in refrigerator or freezer.

Homemade Payday Candy Bars

Ingredients:

1 cup almond flour
1/2 cup Low carb sugar-free peanut butter
1 tsp. vanilla extract
3 tbsp. Swerve confectioners sugar substitute
3 oz. cream cheese softened
2-3 tbsp. Salted or unsalted peanuts
Candy bar silicone mold

Directions:

1. In a mixing bowl, combine the almond flour, peanut butter, vanilla extract and Swerve sweetener. Mix until all ingredients are well combined.
2. Add the cream cheese to the peanut butter mixture, and blend on high until smooth.
3. Place a few peanuts in the bottom of each section of a silicone candy bar mold.
4. Fill each section of the mold with the peanut butter mixture, and pack it in well.
5. Press some peanuts into the top of each candy bar.
6. Place the bars into the freezer to set for at least 30 minutes before serving.

Cucumber and Lime Gummy Snacks

Ingredients:

1 cucumber, peeled
15–20 fresh mint leaves (or 1 Tbsp.)
Juice from 1/2 lime
1.5 tbsps. gelatin powder
1 dash of stevia

Directions:

1. In a blender, blend the cucumber, mint leaves, lime juice, and stevia.
2. Strain the mixture and place the liquid (approx. 1/2 cup or 120 ml liquid) into a small pot on the stove.
3. Heat on medium heat until the liquid starts to simmer.
4. Stir in the gelatin powder (adding a small amount at a time) until it's all dissolved.
5. Strain again to remove any lumps that might have formed.
6. Pour into silicone molds (ice cube trays work well) and refrigerate for 2 hours.

About the Author

Laura Sommers is **The Recipe Lady!**

She is a loving wife and mother who lives on a small farm in Baltimore County, Maryland and has a passion for all things domestic especially when it comes to saving money. She has a profitable eBay business and is a couponing addict. Follow her tips and tricks to learn how to make delicious meals on a budget, save money or to learn the latest life hack!

Visit her Amazon Author Page to see her latest books:

amazon.com/author/laurasommers

Visit the Recipe Lady's blog for even more great recipes:

http://the-recipe-lady.blogspot.com/

Follow the Recipe Lady on **Pinterest**:

http://pinterest.com/therecipelady1

Follow her on Facebook:

https://www.facebook.com/therecipegirl/

Other Books by Laura Sommers

Spaghetti Squash Cookbook

Diabetic Side Dish Cookbook

Diabetic Desserts

Diabetic Cake Cookbook

Printed in Great Britain
by Amazon

29239831R00037